THE
SETTLE to CARLISLE
·A TRIBUTE·

THE SETTLE to CARLISLE

·A TRIBUTE·

Roger Siviter

BLOOMSBURY BOOKS
LONDON

Other Baton Transport Titles

The Metro-land trilogy
by Dennis Edwards and Ron Pigram
Metro Memories
Romance of Metro-land
*The Golden Years of the Metropolitan
Railway*

The Final Link (a pictorial history of
the GW and GC Joint Line)
by Dennis Edwards and Ron Pigram

Down the Line to Dover
by Muriel V. Searle

Down the Line to Hastings
by Brian Jewell

Down the Line to Southend
by Muriel Searle

Author

Roger Siviter, who is an Associate
Member of the Royal Photographic
Society and the author of several railway books, has had a lifelong interest
in railways and for many years has been
a keen photographer of the railway
scene, both in Britain and abroad.

He is a professional musician and
teacher working throughout the
Midlands and lives in Selly Oak,
Birmingham. His previous books
include 'Tempo of Steam', published
by Ian Allan, 'Focus on South African
Steam', 'BR Steam Specials' and
'A Handbook of Railway
Photography', published by David and
Charles.

This edition published 1988 by
Bloomsbury Books an imprint of
Godfrey Cave Associates Limited
42 Bloomsbury Street, London WC1B 3QJ
under license from Baton Transport/Cleveland Press

© Roger Siviter 1984

ISBN 1 870630 26 2

All rights reserved. No part of this
publication may be reproduced, stored
in a retrieval system, or transmitted in
any form or by any means, electronic,
mechanical, photocopying, recording
or otherwise, without the prior
permission of the publisher.

Printed in Yugoslavia

Introduction

When the Settle–Carlisle railway was completed in 1876 by the Midland Railway Company after some six years of work and at a cost of over £3 million, it was regarded as a triumph of Victorian skill and engineering and today, as it probably was then, is regarded as one of the seven wonders of the railway world.

The seventy-three miles from Settle Junction to Carlisle running through the backbone of England – the Pennines – abound with engineering wonders, Ribblehead, Smardale, Arten Gill viaducts, Blea Moor and Rise Hill tunnels to name but a few.

On my many visits to the line over the past years it has always amazed me that each time I seem to find something new to marvel at. And of course the weather and the time of year can dramatically alter the look of the line. What finer sight, as many thousands of people will bear witness, than a splendidly and lovingly restored steam locomotive with a heavy load pounding up to Ais Gill summit on a true winter's day with the fells covered in snow and the exhaust of the locomotive reaching up to the heavens, a sight to behold!

Compare this to a high summer's day in the Eden Valley, with its rich foliage and pasture land, and picture a train speeding through the valley hauled by one of the fine fleet of preserved steam locomotives that work on this one line, another truly beautiful sight.

Both of these scenes are so typical of this line and yet make such a contrast and that for me is the magic of the Settle to Carlisle. All the ingredients are there to make this line probably the finest in the British Isles.

It therefore seemed appropriate that British Rail should have run their last steam train over this route – the famous 'fifteen guinea' special of 11 August 1968. Although steam returned to British Railways in 1971, it was not until 1978 that the first steam specials were to run on this splendid line, passing through some of the most beautiful scenery in England.

Since that first steam special on 25 March 1978 many trips have been run over the line, hauled by a wide variety of locomotives from the diminutive 0–6–0 *Maude* to the mighty *Duchess of Hamilton*.

The pictorial section of this book recreates a journey on the line hauled by these beautiful locomotives showing them passing through magnificent scenery, crossing high viaducts and in the many splendid locations of which the line abounds. This section is divided into three main parts – Settle Junction to Garsdale, Garsdale to Appleby and Appleby to Carlisle, these being the three principal legs of the journey of the Cumbrian Mountain trains on the Settle Junction–Carlisle section. There is a detailed map at the beginning of each section and the numbers marked on it correspond with the photographs in the book. Also featured are the British Rail service trains of the last few years hauled by a wide variety of diesel locomotives including the type 40s and 45s (which seem so much at home on the line).

Sadly the line is under threat of closure. It is to be hoped that this does not happen. Indeed it would be a very sad day if this ever came about.

In conclusion, I should like to thank all the people involved in the preparation of this book. To the photographers who very kindly allowed me to choose pictures from their collections, to Joan Wappett for the typing, to my wife Christina for the maps and help with the layout and to my publisher, Ray Green of Baton Press, for allowing complete freedom in the choice of material and layout. To Bernard Staite and the Steam Locomotive Operators' Association (SLOA) for running such splendid trains which are enjoyed by so many people and to the railwaymen (professional and amateur) who make it all possible. Last but not least to the 'Friends of the Settle to Carlisle Line Association' for their sterling efforts to save this splendid line.

NOTE Unless otherwise specified all photographs were taken by the author.

Part One
Settle Junction to Garsdale

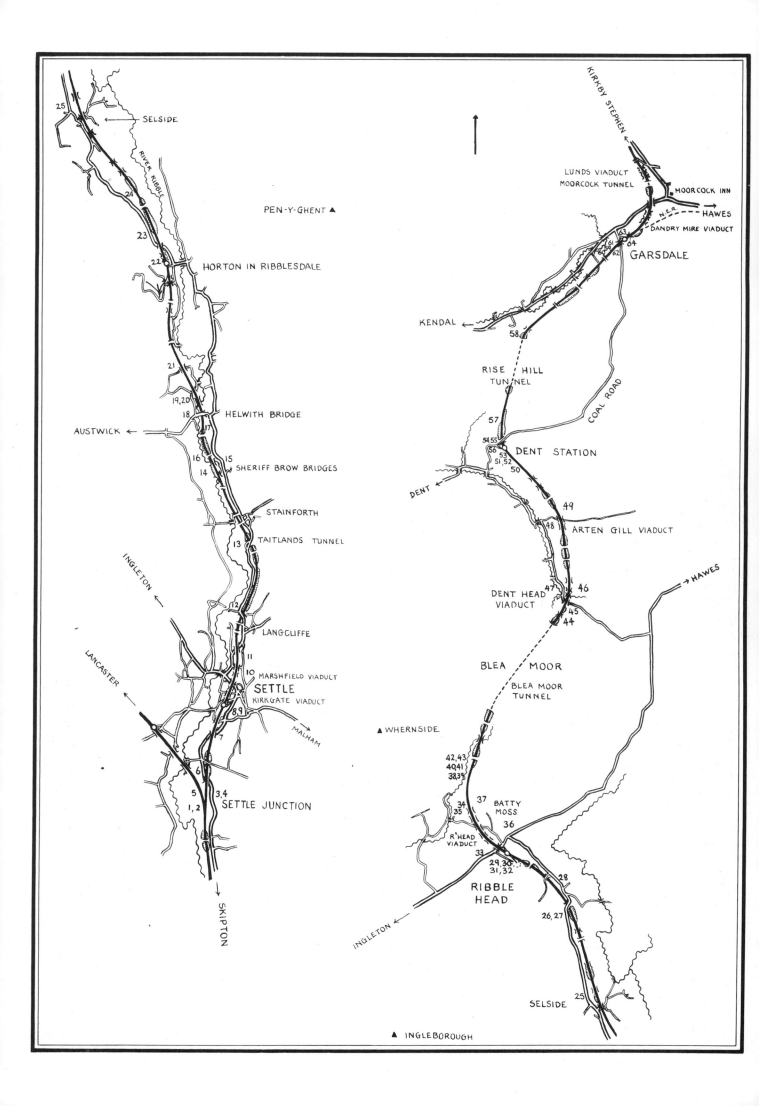

25

← SELSIDE

RIVER RIBBLE

24

23

22

PEN-Y-GHENT ▲

HORTON IN RIBBLESDALE

21

19,20

18

AUSTWICK ←

17

16   15

14   SHERIFF BROW BRIDGES

HELWITH BRIDGE

STAINFORTH

13   TAITLANDS TUNNEL

INGLETON

12

LANGCLIFFE

11

LANCASTER

10   MARSHFIELD VIADUCT

SETTLE

KIRKGATE VIADUCT

8,9

7   MALHAM →

6

5   3,4

1,2   SETTLE JUNCTION

SKIPTON

KIRKBY STEPHEN

LUNDS VIADUCT
MOORCOCK TUNNEL

MOORCOCK INN

N.E.R.   HAWES →

63   DANDRY MIRE VIADUCT

61   64

62   GARSDALE

KENDAL ←

58

RISE HILL
TUNNEL

COAL ROAD

57

54,55

56   53   DENT STATION

51,52

50

DENT ←

49

48   ARTEN GILL VIADUCT

47   46   HAWES →

45

DENT HEAD
VIADUCT   44

BLEA   MOOR

BLEA MOOR
TUNNEL

▲ WHERNSIDE

42,43

40,41

38,39

37   BATTY
34   MOSS

35

36

R'HEAD
VIADUCT   33

29,30

31,32   28

RIBBLE
HEAD

INGLETON ←

26,27

SELSIDE   25

▲ INGLEBOROUGH

Settle Junction to Garsdale

The route begins at the box and signals about 13 miles north of Skipton where the line divides, one line turning northwest over the River Ribble to Carnforth and the other, the subject of this book, continuing north into Settle, where the line runs through the centre of the town over a series of viaducts.

The energetic can enjoy the view of Settle and its railway station from the flagpole on the cliff on the east side. But those with less energy may stay on the train whose rails thread northward through the valley, closely intertwined with the river and the road – the B6479 for Horton-in-Ribblesdale. The track skirts the foot of a great crag near Langcliffe, then nips through Taitlands Tunnel. After about a mile it crosses the river by a skew bridge near Sherwood House on Sherriff Brow, then crosses back again, to rise through a gloomy gorge and break out among the boulders at Helwith Bridge, where the inn is noted for its peacocks. Photographers have recently been using this location, as the telephone poles that hitherto marred the view have been removed.

The valley widens at Helwith Bridge to give an expansive view westwards across water meadows to where quarries rise up the far side at Foredale. At the end of this stretch, the B6479 road zigzags through Horton-in-Ribblesdale to rejoin the line at the side of the station. In this village, rail enthusiasts vie with potholers and walkers coming down off Pen-y-Ghent to the east. The station still has its box and signals, and sidings that served the branch from Beecroft quarries.

The road passes under the line to the west side and, immediately after, can be seen a fallen bush lying on the embankment. This spot is known to enthusiasts as 'Horton Field No 1'. The next field is 'Horton Field No 2', naturally. The line continues to rise with a steady gradient through wide rolling moorlands. At Selside there was a signal box, but all that now remains is the nameboard fixed to a barn. Between the track and the road a line of Midland Railway cottages display the characteristically steep dormers of these terraced company dwellings.

After a couple of miles the road crosses back to the east and passes another line of Midland's cottages. These are 'Salt Lake Cottages', built on the site of one of the construction shanty towns which was given the name of Salt Lake City. At the approach to the junction with the Hawes–Ingleton road can be glimpsed Ribblehead Viaduct, an engineering miracle of twenty-four arches, a hundred feet high and 440 yards long which spans Batty Moss and has survived many years of appalling weather. The former station here also used to serve as a chapel and a meteorological station. The quarry hard by sends its trains over the viaduct to the sidings by Blea Moor box to reverse for the journey south, and to link the spur it was necessary to take up the down platform, and this provides an interesting descent from the train for the many hill walkers using the monthly 'Dales Rail' specials.

At a thousand feet above sea level, the signal box for Blea Moor Tunnel must be the most desolate in the land; the house alongside was once occupied but now lies empty, and signal men commute for their shifts. The water tower which stood on the west side is now demolished. This long tunnel itself is a major feat of engineering, helped by the early use of dynamite; at the north end can be seen the banks and trackbeds of spoil tips. The train emerges into dark forestry plantations, and soars out on to Dent Head Viaduct and then Arten Gill, a tall slender viaduct built of 'black' limestone. The gradient here is easier, as the line skirts the head of Dent Dale where the hillside is lined with pallisades, to prevent the winter snows from drifting onto the line.

Dent Station signal box still stands, though its signals have gone, their only relic being a painted white panel on the bridge – a 'back plate' for a semaphore. This bridge carries the famous 'coal road' from Lea Yeat in Dent Dale to Garsdale and is not a route for the fainthearted. The station building at 1,155 feet, the highest in England, has been taken over by a school as an outdoor pursuits centre, and the only trains that stop here are the 'Dales Rail' specials and the occasional run-pasts by SLOA specials. Beyond the bridge, a stream crosses the line in a piped channel. The cutting's northern end is guarded by a conspicuous lone pine, overlooking the plantations on Dodderham Moss.

The line now runs over Cowgill Beck on embankments and plunges into Rise Hill tunnel, to emerge again a mile further on, in Garsdale Valley, to run along the hillside parallel with the road. There used to be water troughs here, steam heated to prevent freezing, but steam specials now take water in the station, on the approach to which can be seen signals and a row of Midland's terraced cottages on the left, where the line crosses the end of the 'coal road'.

1. *Above* No 34092 *City of Wells*, former Southern Railway West Country Class Pacific, storms through Settle Junction on 3 December 1983 with a northbound *Cumbrian Mountain Pullman (CMP)*. Where this photograph was taken is just south of Settle Junction signal box, virtually at the start of the long climb to Ais Gill summit some 24 miles to the north.

The first leg of the journey from Carnforth to Hellifield (where No 34092 took charge) would have been worked by one of the fleet of steam locomotives shedded at Carnforth. BRIAN DOBBS

2. *Top right* This photograph, taken at the same place as the previous picture, shows LMS Class 5 No 5407, a 4-6-0 locomotive built in the 1930s to Sir William Stainier's design and now beautifully restored, heading for Hellifield with the bottom leg of the northbound CMP from Carnforth to Hellifield where *City of Wells* will take charge for the journey to Carlisle. 13 November 1982.

3. *Bottom right* A good view of the Midland Railway signal box at Settle Junction with LNER Pacific No 4498 *Sir Nigel Gresley* as it crosses the junction heading the Carnforth to Leeds portion of the *Trans Pennine Pullman* on 26 September 1981.

The line for Carlisle can be seen on the right.

4. *Top* No 5407 blasts out at Settle Junction and heads northwestwards for Carnforth with the southbound *Cumbrian Mountain Express* (CME) on 14 September 1983.

The left hand tracks are the S & C main line which within a few hundred yards diverge northwards towards the town of Settle.

5. *Bottom* Class 45/1 No 45126 coasts into Settle Junction with a return Carlisle–Derby special train on 3 March 1984. The divergence of tracks is seen clearly here with the lines to Carnforth, on the left side, veering away to the northwest.
K. J. C. JACKSON

6. *Top* Coronation Pacific No 46229 *Duchess of Hamilton* leaves the Carnforth line behind as it climbs away from Settle Junction and heads for Carlisle on 28 May 1983. This beautiful engine is shedded at the National Railway Museum at York and is arguably the most popular locomotive running over this route.
K. J. C. JACKSON

7. *Bottom* On a wet 30 April 1983 *City of Wells* is seen climbing the 1 in 100 gradient up to Settle with a northbound CMP. The location is about half a mile south of Settle Station, where the A65 road to Kendal cuts under the line.
DON TAGGART

8. *Top left* No 34092 sets off from a temporary stop at Settle station on a very wet 2 May 1983 and passes the Midland Railway signal box (now out of use) with a southbound CMP. After arrival at Hellifield the bottom leg of the journey to Carnforth will be completed by the former Somerset & Dorset 2-8-0 No 13809.

9. *Bottom left* Business looks brisk at Settle as Class 45/1 No 45115 draws to a stop with the 1600 Leeds–Carlisle on 27 July 1983. Sadly, when this picture was taken there were only two trains in each direction – morning and early evening. Note the fine Victorian gothic style architecture of the station buildings and the splendid chimneys. K. J. C. JACKSON

10. *Top right* 4-6-0 No 850 *Lord Nelson* climbs away from Settle on 25 February 1984 with the northbound CMP. At this point it is crossing the main A65 trunk route to Kendal and the Lake District.

In this view is Settle parish church which contains one of the two memorial plaques dedicated to those who died while building the line. K. J. C. JACKSON

11. *Bottom right* Coasting through the pleasantly rural meadowlands just to the north of the ancient town of Settle on 17 May 1980 is the splendid North British 0-6-0 *Maude* bound for the Liverpool & Manchester 150th Anniversary celebrations at Rainhill. This locomotive is shedded at the Scottish RPS society depot at Falkirk and on this occasion had made its way south via the Glasgow & South Western route to Carlisle and then over the Settle & Carlisle line to Hellifield, thence to Rainhill via Blackburn and Manchester.

12. *Above* The impressive limestone cliffs at Langcliffe (a mile or so to the north of Settle) dominate the scene as Brush Class 31/1 No 31174 heads south on 24 August 1983 with the 1635 Carlisle–Leeds.
DAVID WILCOCK

13. *Top right* The celebrated LNER Pacific No 4472 *Flying Scotsman* performing yeoman service on the S & C route, at work climbing northwards out of Settle at Taitlands just south of Stainforth. The ruling grade here is 1 in a 100 and the sixty-year-old veteran seems to be taking it well in her stride. The date is 22 June 1983.

14. *Bottom right* Heading the northbound *Santa Steam Special* on 28 December 1983 is LMS Class 5 No 5305, beautifully restored at Hull by the Humberside Locomotive Preservation Group. This train which is especially run for the 'younger generation' will stop at Appleby where Father Christmas will entrain to distribute presents.

The location is Sherriff Brow in the Stainforth Gorge, some three miles to the north of Settle. K. J. C. JACKSON

15. *Top left* A rare visitor to the S & C is BR Class 9F No 92220 *Evening Star*, here seen crossing the River Ribble at Batty Wood on the 30 September 1978 with a special train from the West Riding of Yorkshire to Appleby for a memorial service to the late Bishop Eric Treacy who was surely the doyen of railway photographers.

16. *Bottom left* The same location as the previous picture but this time viewed from the western side on 15 May 1982. The train is the northbound CMP hauled by King Arthur Class 4-6-0 of the Southern Railway No 777 *Sir Lamiel*. D. J. O'ROURKE

17. *Top right* After crossing the Ribble at Batty Wood the line climbs towards Helwith Bridge, closely following the course of the river, and in this view just south of Helwith Bridge we see Class 31/1 31239 on 23 April 1983 with the northbound morning Leeds–Carlisle train. The buildings on the right are part of a quarry and there are further quarries to the north of Helwith Bridge on the west side of the line at Foredale. Note also the stone wall, so typical of the Yorkshire Dales.
DAVID WILCOCK

18. *Bottom right* The River Ribble provides the foreground for Southern Railway 4-6-0 No 850 at Helwith Bridge with the northbound CMP on 27 November 1982.

19. *Top left* A few hundred yards to the north of Helwith Bridge the line again crosses the River Ribble. This splendid view shows *Lord Nelson*, this time with a southbound train on 5 August 1981.

Overlooking the scene is Pen-y-Ghent, one of the three tremendous peaks which dominate this area, the other two being Ingleborough and Wernside. CHRIS MILNER

20. *Bottom left* The sheep are grazing peacefully as LNER K1 2-6-0 leaves Helwith Bridge behind and forges northwards towards Ribblehead with the SLOA Pullman set on 20 March 1983.

This train, the *Northumbrian Mountain Pullman*, when it arrives at Carlisle will reverse and then proceed to Newcastle and Middlesborough where it will terminate. TOM HEAVYSIDE

21. *Top right* LMS Jubilee 4-6-0 No 5690 *Leander* piloted by 5 MT 5407 on the northbound CMP on 20 May 1982. The train is seen here threading the flat meadowland between Helwith Bridge and Horton-in-Ribblesdale. K. J. C. JACKSON

22. *Bottom right* No 46229 storms up the 1 in 100 at Horton-in-Ribblesdale, past the sidings for Beecroft Quarry with a northbound CMP on 12 March 1983. At this time the Midland Railway signal box was still in use.

23. *Top left* The 1 March 1980 was a glorious day and yet there is just a solitary car on the B6479 as Class 5 No 5305 climbs up from Horton-in-Ribblesdale Station with a northbound train. At this popular spot there is usually a fair crowd of people to view and photograph the northbound steam trains and the road is very often chock-a-block with cars. The weather forecasters obviously got it wrong for this particular weekend!

24. *Bottom left* A few hundred yards northwards from the previous picture is this spot which enthusiasts call Horton Field No 2, which provides a splendid grandstand from which to photograph northbound trains.
   The date is 13 November 1982 and the locomotive is the *City of Wells* with a northbound CMP.

25. *Top right* Climbing past the Midland Railway cottages at Selside on Sunday 20 March 1983 is K1 2-6-0 No 2005 with the northbound *Northumbrian Mountain Pullman*.
   Also note the cars on the B6479 in the foreground obviously chasing the train.

26. *Bottom right* No 35028 *Clan Line*, a Merchant Navy Class Pacific of the Southern Railway makes a fine sight as it climbs through Selside with the northbound *Citadel Express* from Euston to Carlisle on 23 September 1978. J. H. COOPER-SMITH

27. *Top left* The clouds create dramatic shadows on the side of Pen-y-Ghent as *City of Wells* coasts down through Selside with a southbound train 3 May 1982.

28. *Bottom left* There is snow on the top of Whernside as Class 47/4 No 47444 races southwards with a diverted Glasgow–Euston express on 2 April 1983. The cottages in the picture were built by the Midland Railway for their employees. DAVID WILCOCK

29. *Top right* All that now remains at Ribblehead Station is the up platform and its buildings. The down platform was removed in recent years in order to put a line in to Ribblehead Quarry. This line can be seen in the foreground as *City of Wells* runs through the station with a southbound CMP on 10 December 1983.

30. *Bottom right* Class 25/2 No 25247 with a goods train loaded by dumper truck at Ribblehead Quarry on Tuesday 8 February 1983. After being loaded it then proceeds over Ribblehead Viaduct to gain the up line at Blea Moor. It then returns southwards. DAVID WILCOCK

31. *Top left* Low sunlight and a dramatic sky combine to produce a memorable picture of A4 Pacific No 4498 *Sir Nigel Gresley* as it climbs towards Ribblehead or Batty Moss Viaduct with a northbound CMP on 28 November 1981.

This splendid locomotive built in the mid 1930s to Gresley's design was a regular performer on the S & C until it went into works for a major overhaul. K. J. C. JACKSON

32. *Bottom left* *Duchess of Hamilton* proceeding south with the CMP on the 5 November 1983; the train has just left Ribblehead Viaduct and is approaching Ribblehead Station. The wreath on the smoke-box door is to commemorate Poppy Day.

So typical of late Autumn in this part of the world is the fact that Whernside is shrouded in mist.

33. *Top right* *Flying Scotsman* heads north across Ribblehead Viaduct on 3 September 1983 with the *Mainline Railway Special*. This view, taken from the south-west and looking towards Whernside, shows the scaffolding from which reinforcing work is done on the viaduct. K. J. C. JACKSON

34. *Bottom right* This view of Ribblehead Viaduct was taken from the north-west showing Pen-y-Ghent in the background. *Sir Nigel Gresley* provides the motive power for this northbound train on 28 November 1981. This splendid viaduct has 24 spans and is 440 yards long. J. H. COOPER-SMITH

35. *Top left* An unidentified Class 25 heads south over Ribblehead Viaduct with a train from Ribblehead Quarry on 7 September 1982.

36. *Bottom left* The classic combination of Midland compound 4-4-0 locomotive No 1000 and Jubilee class 4-6-0 No 5690 *Leander* silhouetted on Ribblehead Viaduct on a very wintry 12 February 1982. The train is a southbound CMP.

37. *Above* K1 2-6-0 No 2005 is caught in dramatic silhouette pose as it heads northwards off Ribblehead Viaduct and heads for Carlisle. The date is 20 March 1983. J. H. COOPER-SMITH

Overleaf

38. *Top left* Framed by splendid semaphore signals as it approaches Blea Moor is 4-6-0 No 850 *Lord Nelson* with a northbound CMP on 27 November 1982. ROGER HILL

39. *Bottom left* A similar view to the previous picture, but who could resist this fine portrait of *Duchess of Hamilton* as it climbs up to Blea Moor with the northbound CME on 29 October 1983. Ingleborough is the peak dominating the background.
J. H. COOPER-SMITH

40. *Top right* Blea Moor with its loops and sidings which are still used today for reversal of the quarry trains and for standby locomotives.
Gentle back lighting silhouettes Ingleborough and highlights the special northbound train hauled by Class 25 25035 and Class 31 No 31102. The date is 5 November 1983.

41. *Bottom right* The 5 February 1983 is very well remembered by all those who were out on that dreadful day. It was the first run over the S & C by the Midland Compound No 1000 coupled to No 5690 *Leander*. Because of the dreadful weather the train was considerably delayed and in consequence most people waited for a long time in appalling weather conditions (a friend who was with the author actually suffered from frost bite!). Many photographers failed to get any pictures at all that day but we are lucky to have this fine portrait of a classic pair of locomotives as they head northwards through the snow and past Blea Moor box.
D. J. O'ROURKE

42. *Above* This scene, from the occupation bridge at the northern end of Blea Moor sidings, shows No 46229 storming through with a northbound train complete with *Thames–Clyde Express* headboard, the classic LMS train of the 30s and 40s over this route. 26 March 1983. J. H. COOPER-SMITH

43. *Top right* The diverted 0810 Glasgow–Euston, framed by semaphore signals as it hastens its journey southwards on 2 April 1983, hauled by Class 47/4 No 47440. Note the beautiful stonework in the typical Midland Railway occupation bridge, just south of Blea Moor Tunnel. DAVID WILCOCK

44. *Bottom right* Jubilee class 4-6-0 *Leander* leaves the northern portals of Blea Moor Tunnel and heads up through Dentdale with a northbound special on 16 October 1982. The plantations of conifer trees now dominate the head of this valley. KEN BULL

45. *Above* A very wintry scene at Dent Head Viaduct as Class 5 4-6-0 No 5305 heads south with the *Cumbrian Mountain Express* on 22 March 1980. J. H. COOPER-SMITH

46. *Right* Class 47/4 No 47424 crossing Dent Head Viaduct after leaving the 2,629 yards long Blea Moor Tunnel with the diverted 0750 Manchester–Glasgow train on 2 April 1983. This great limestone-built viaduct has 10 spans and is 197 yards long, with a maximum height of 100 feet.

Overleaf

47. *Left* This unusual view of Dent Head Viaduct is taken from the western side of the line and shows LMS Class 5 No 4767 *George Stephenson* with a northbound special on 21 February 1981. From this angle the viaduct looks more impressive than usual and clearly shows the beautiful lines of the arches. CHRIS MILNER

48. *Top right* The graceful Arten Gill Viaduct is a mile or so to the north of that of Dent Head. This picture, taken from Stone Houses, shows the 11 spans of the beautiful 220-yard-long viaduct – a fine memorial to Victorian engineering.

The train, which looks diminutive in this setting, is a northbound CMP hauled by 4-6-0 No 777 *Sir Lamiel* and the date is 15 May 1982.

49. *Bottom right* The deserted shepherd's cottage adds foreground depth to this picture of 4-6-0 *Lord Nelson* crossing Arten Gill Viaduct with the northbound CME on 25 February 1984. In the background are the snow flecked hills of Whernside.

Previous pages
50. *Top left* A classic locomotive in a classic setting: LNER Pacific No 4472 *Flying Scotsman* approaching Dent Station with the northbound *Mainline Railways* special on 3 September 1983. Arten Gill Viaduct is in the background on the right. Note the snow fence barriers, a necessary protection for a line in this part of the country, for at an elevation of around 1,000 feet Dent is the highest station in England. Also to be seen is the track bed of the down siding which was removed in 1982. CHRIS MILNER

51. *Bottom left* The dilapidated signal box at Dent remains as a visual reminder of the Midland Railway, and in this photograph overlooks preserved English Electric Class 40 No D200 as it rounds the curve into Dent Station on 24 August 1983, with the 1600 Leeds–Carlisle train.

52. *Top right* Down platform and sidings at Dent shown to advantage in this portrait of a southbound CME hauled by No 850 *Lord Nelson* on 31 July 1980. At this time the signalling was still in place. J. GORDON BLEARS

53. *Bottom right* Dent Station taken on May 22 1982, by which date the signals and brackets had been removed as well as the down sidings.
   The southbound CMP is hauled here by 4-6-0 No 777 *Sir Lamiel*.

54. *Above* One of the first special trains to run over the S & C was the *Aire–Eden Limited* from Nottingham to Carlisle on 21 October 1978. It was hauled from Leeds to Carlisle by *Sir Nigel Gresley* seen here about to leave Dent after pausing for a photo stop. The photograph was taken from the road bridge at the northern end of the station.

55. *Top right* Taken from a similar angle as the previous picture but some four and a half years later, on 22 June 1983. All the sidings and signalling have been removed and the box is out of use. It still makes an interesting view as the northbound CMP leaves through the station hauled by *Flying Scotsman*.

56. *Bottom right* Class 5 4-6-0 No 5407 making a fine sight through Dent with the southbound CME on 2 September 1981. The bridge carries the famous coal road to Garsdale Station.

57 *Above* North of Dent is Rise Hill Tunnel, 1,213 yards in length and originally known as Black Moss. In this view of a southbound CMP hauled by *Flying Scotsman* the train has left the tunnel and is approaching the cutting to the north of Dent. The date is 29 June 1983.

J. H. COOPER-SMITH

58. *Top right* Nos 1000 and 5690 caught by the camera on a snowy 12 February 1983 as they approach the northern end of Rise Hill Tunnel with a southbound CMP.
DAVID WILCOCK

59. *Bottom right* Nos 1000 and 5690 as they leave Garsdale on 12 February 1983 and approach the site of Garsdale water troughs (the highest in England). These troughs were steam heated to prevent freezing. BRIAN DOBBS

60. *Above* On 29/30 January 1983 the Steam Locomotive Operators Association (SLOA) held their Annual General Meeting at Carlisle, when one of the highlights of the weekend was a Sunday trip over the S & C, hauled by *Flying Scotsman*. The special train is seen here leaving Garsdale for the south. Cottages in the background were built by the Midland Railway for their employees.

61. *Right* Semaphore signalling and signal box still in use at Garsdale as LMS Class 5 4-6-0 No 5407 sets out from the water stop and heads south for Hellifield and Carnforth with the CMP. The date is 24 August 1983. DEREK G. SMITH

62. *Above* Back lighting on 29 October 1983 accentuates the northbound CME hauled by *Duchess of Hamilton* as it coasts round the curve into Garsdale and past the site of the up sidings which have long since been removed. After arrival the locomotive will take water and then perform a series of run pasts with the train for the benefit of the passengers. It will then head north up the final three miles of heavy gradients to Ais Gill Summit and then coast down the Mallerstang Valley to Appleby and through the Eden Valley to Carlisle. KEN BULL

63. *Right* When Sir William Stanier designed the Coronation Pacific class of locomotives in 1937 its primary task was to haul expresses on the West Coast Main Line. This is now performed by electric locomotives but fortunately *Duchess of Hamilton* survives to work specials over the S & C route, as can be seen in this action portrait of No 46229 leaving Garsdale on 28 March 1981 with the southbound CME.

Out of Garsdale the gradients to the south are undulating as far as Blea Moor, but from there onwards it is all down grade to Settle junction. KEN BULL

64. *Above Flying Scotsman* pictured at Garsdale Station with the southbound SLOA
special on 30 January 1983. The train is on the down platform to allow diverted up west
coast main line trains to run through the station. For the last few years there have been
Sunday diversions over this route. DAVID WILCOCK

Part Two
Garsdale to Appleby

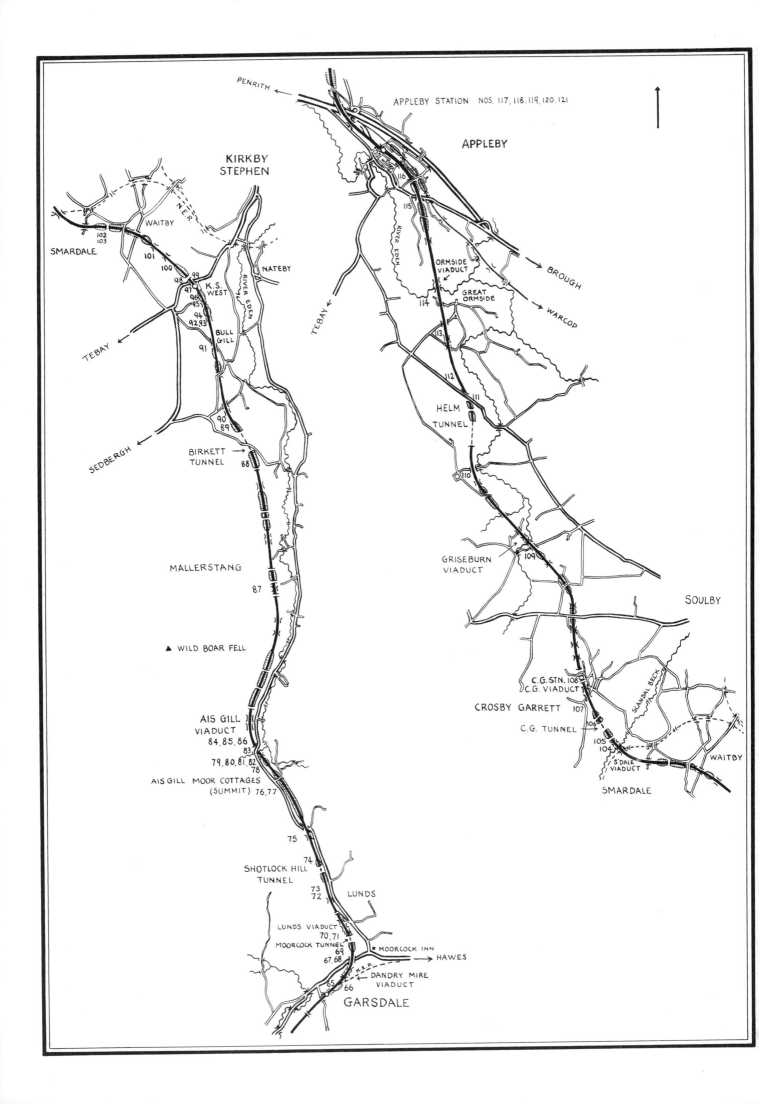

Garsdale to Appleby

Garsdale station used to be called Hawes Junction and the track bed of the Hawes branch can still be seen swinging eastwards on leaving the station. To the left are a working signal box and the round pit of the former turntable, where once the shed pilot spun round in a gale; in consequence, the turntable was later protected by a wall of sleepers.

After Garsdale the line crosses Dandry Mire by an impressive viaduct, past a chapel, a line of Midland cottages and the Moorcock Inn, then enters the valley northwards for Ais Gill. A brief foray through Moorcock tunnel takes the line out on to Lunds Viaduct, now reinforced with tie-bars, then under Grisedale Crossing footbridge conveying a right of way. The hillsides round here are a network of footpaths, leading to an isolated chapel or a YHA hostel. The road runs close to the east side of the tracks and rises abruptly as the line ducks into Shotlock Hill Tunnel. After a short distance, the line climbs over the road at Shaw Paddock, hard by a farm whose doors are painted a cheerful red.

The track ascends through a long shallow cutting as far as the summit and past Ais Gill Moor cottages, noted for afternoon high teas and a collection of interesting bird-life. There is a particularly good view of the 'Long Drag' from the occupation bridge at the back. Once there were a box and signals at the summit, controlling a siding for a pilot engine, but all that now remains are a line of telephone poles and an altitude board proclaiming the height at 1,169 feet. As the line runs out onto the watershed it passes a waterfall on the right, a spectacular sight when in winter spate.

Looking northwards, passengers will see a road bridge crossing the line to drop steeply down the valley and, behind this, dominating the pass, the distinctive two-tier skyline of Wild Boar Fell. A short distance after this bridge the line crosses its namesake by Ais Gill Viaduct and passes under the wooden Hangman's Bridge, named after a suicide, and for the next few miles there will be a splendid view to the east of Mallerstang Edge and the River Eden. Just before Birkett Tunnel can be glimpsed Pendragon Castle, supposedly built by King Arthur's father, guarding the valley as it has for centuries.

Birkett Common marks a change from moorland to pasture, and soon the line is skipping through wooded cuttings and over embankments at Bull Gill, then over the A685 running from Tebay to Kirkby Stephen Station, which still operates a cluster of semaphores. A mile nearer Kirkby Stephen, this road crosses the now-abandoned NE line, which ran from Tebay to Kirkby Stephen Junction and then either to Newcastle or to Appleby and Penrith. Only the short branch from Appleby to the army range at Warcop survives. As the Ais Gill line swings westward it crosses the disused tracks of the Tebay line and runs over Scandal Beck, a tributary of the Eden, by means of Smardale Viaduct, tie-bars now reinforcing the grey limestone.

On leaving the wooded ravine, a short tunnel brings the train above the picturesque Crosby Garrett, where the railway route soars high over village lanes and fords. The line now snakes north over gently rolling pastures, over Griseburn Viaduct and past the site of the Griseburn ballast sidings, where there is still a box, in an immaculate state of preservation. From here the line continues past Breaks Hall, until it plunges into Helm Tunnel.

Emerging from the tunnel by Helm village, passengers can appreciate the full sweep of the Eden Valley and beyond to the great wall of hills that form part of the Pennine Way, its highest point being Cross Fell. Sometimes here can be seen a curious cloud formation like a black bar, created by the 'Helm Wind', running the length of the valley. The winds can be so strong here that an anerometer set at High Cup Nick was blown from its moorings.

The line descends past the disused station at Great Ormside and crosses the River Eden by an elegant viaduct, then rises again. About half a mile before Appleby Station is a right of way crossing the line by the Express Dairy, where steam specials take on water. There used to be a private siding here for the 'Milk to London' service. The ground frame box that worked the siding has now disappeared.

Arriving at Appleby, the train passes a former goods shed on the left and just past the site of the water tower on the right is the name picked out in white stones on the embankment. The station buildings on the left carry a memorial plaque to the 'Railway Bishop', the Reverend Eric Treacy, Bishop of Wakefield, who died on the platform on 13 May 1978, waiting to photograph the locomotive *Evening Star*.

65. *Top left* Midland Railway signal box at Garsdale on 13 May 1983 as Class 31/4 No 31411 coasts into the station with the afternoon Carlisle to Leeds train. But this train will not stop here, its next stop being Settle. The only trains that now stop at the intermediate stations between Settle, Appleby and Carlisle are the 'Dales Rails' trains, a DMU service which is run once a month especially for walkers and climbers. Garsdale was once known as Hawes Juction and the remains of the trackbed of the North Eastern line to Hawes can be seen at the end of the train. DAVID WILCOCK

66. *Bottom left* Following the Ayr Railfair & Sou' Wester of Saturday 12 November 1983, at which *Flying Scotsman* was one of the stars, the locomotive then worked south via the S & C route on the following Monday. It is seen here entering Garsdale having just crossed over Garsdale or Dandry Mire Viaduct.

The well of the old turntable can be seen on the left edge of the picture and the sidings on the up line are a reminder of more affluent times at this once busy junction. Note also the chapel nestling in the valley and the Midland cottages to the right of the line. DAVID WILCOCK

67. *Above* A4 Pacific *Sir Nigel Gresley* makes a fine sight as it heads northwards away from Garsdale and over the Dandry Mire Viaduct. Also known as Moorcock Viaduct, it is 227 yards long and has 12 spans. This view, taken on 28 November 1981, is from the A684 Sedburgh to Hawes Road. CHRIS MILNER

Overleaf

68. *Left* The chapel on the Sedburgh road acts as a frame for K1 2-6-0 No 2005 as it crosses Dandry Mire Viaduct with a northbound special on 20 March 1983. K. J. C. JACKSON

69. *Top right* No 46229 storms away from Dandry Mire Viaduct in fine style with the northbound CMP on 20 February 1982.

Just above and to the left of the front end of the locomotive can be seen the alignment of the old North Eastern Railway branch to Hawes.

70. *Bottom right* A portrait of 4-6-0 *Lord Nelson* running out of Moorcock Tunnel and crossing Lunds Viaduct with the northbound CMP on 27 November 1982, the back lighting creating beautiful patterns on the fells. ROGER HILL

71. *Above* This view of Lunds Viaduct was taken in the summer of 1982 and shows *Duchess of Hamilton* heading northwards with the CME.

The fells of Abbotside Common provide a pleasant background to this very summery scene. DAVID WILCOCK

72. *Right* Class K1 No 2005 climbing up to Shotlock Hill Tunnel on 20 March 1983 with the *Northumbrian Mountain Pullman*. Just south of here is Grisedale Crossing where the Midland Railway cottages were originally built for linesmen on the Settle & Carlisle.

Overleaf

73. *Top left* Looking as elegant as ever, Jubilee Class 4-6-0 No 5690 *Leander* photographed to the south of Shotlock Hill Tunnel on the 16 October 1982 heading the northbound *Leander Express*, with steam haulage from Leeds–Carlisle and then back to Hellifield. The train originated in Norwich so the passengers will be getting in some good 'track mileage'.

74. *Bottom left* Class 9F 2-10-0 *Evening Star* bursts out of the short tunnel at Shotlock Hill with *The Bishop Treacy* special train run on 30 September 1978. The train stopped at Appleby where a special memorial service was held for the late 'Railway Bishop'. D. J. O'ROURKE

75. *Top right* A panoramic view of Abbotside Common with *Lord Nelson* climbing up to Ais Gill Summit with a northbound special on 27 November 1982.

This location is half way between Shotlock Hill Tunnel and the summit, namely Shaw Paddock, where the B6259 to Kirkby Stephen cuts under the line.

76. *Bottom right* Ais Gill Summit taken on a beautiful summer's day (10 August 1982). *Duchess of Hamilton* with a northbound special has just passed the signal box and is approaching the summit board, announcing the fact that it is 1169 feet above sea level. By this time the sidings on the down line for the pilot engines had been lifted and all that remains is the track bed. BRIAN DOBBS

Previous pages

77. *Top left* On 2 April 1983 the Ais Gill Summit board is still in place. Now the signal box has been removed, and has been restored to its former glory at Butterley by the Midland Railway Trust.

The train battling through the blizzard is the diverted 1043 Euston–Glasgow hauled by Class 47/4 No 47540. Contrast this scene with picture 46 which was taken only a few hours earlier on the same day; it will be seen how quickly weather conditions can change on the S & C line.

78. *Bottom left* With a misty Wild Boar Fell dominating the background, *Duchess of Hamilton* throws out a fine exhaust as it climbs up the last few yards to Ais Gill Summit with a southbound CME on 5 November 1983.

79. *Right* Hull based Class 5 No 5305 nearing Ais Gill Summit with a southbound CME on 22 March 1980. The locomotive seems to be in fine fettle after the tremendous climb from Appleby to the summit, a distance of some 19 miles at around gradients of 1 in 100. The semaphore signals and box were still in use at this time. J. H. COOPER-SMITH

80. *Above* In latter years perhaps the most unique sight on the S & C has been the veteran North British 0-6-0 *Maude* caught here as it climbs to Ais Gill Summit bound for the 150th anniversary celebrations at Rainhill on 17 May 1980.

81. *Top right* Ais Gill Summit on a true winter's day – 30 January 1983 – as *Flying Scotsman* climbs the last few yards to the summit with the SLOA AGM special train. Winter brings out all of the majesty and splendour of this most famous railway route.

82. *Bottom right* After crossing under the road bridge which carries the B6259 to Kirkby Stephen LNER V2 2-6-2 No 4771 *Green Arrow* has the summit in its sight as it hauls the *Norfolkman* towards the south on Easter Monday (27 March) 1978. It was the first southbound steam working over this route since the famous 'Fifteen Guinea Special' of 11 August 1968. The first revived outward northbound steam working, hauled by *Green Arrow*, was on the previous Saturday (25 March 1978).

83. *Above* The same train as in the previous picture and taken from the same place, only now as a three-quarter view as it forges up to Ais Gill Summit. Easter 1978 was exceptionally cold and flecks of snow can still be seen on Wild Boar Fell.

84. *Top right* LMS Class 5 4-6-0 No 5407 in pristine condition with steam to spare, caught broadside, forging up the Mallerstang Valley to Ais Gill with a southbound CME on a beautiful late summer day (2 September) in 1981.

85. *Bottom right* Ais Gill Viaduct is only 87 yards long but here provides a splendid setting for No 1000 and *Leander* as they climb up to the summit on 12 February 1983 with a southbound CMP. D. C. CHANDLER

Top: No 34092 *City of Wells* approaches Settle Junction with the
Carnforth–Hellifield portion of the northbound *Cumbrian
Mountain Pullman*. 29 May 1982.

Above: No 46229 climbs up to Ais Gill summit with southbound
CME. 5 November 1983. CHRISTINA SIVITER

Top: Class 47/4 No 47508 approaches Culgaith level-crossing with the diverted 1110 Glasgow–Euston train on Sunday 22 April 1984.

Above: Class 45/0 No 45020 glows in the evening sunshine as it crosses Ais Gill Viaduct with the 1635 Carlisle–Leeds. 24 April 1984.

Above: No 60009 approaches Lazonby station with the southbound
CME on 24 April 1984. CHRISTINA SIVITER

Opposite Top: No 5407 and *Leander* cross Ribblehead Viaduct on 29 May 1982 with a northbound special.

Above: Preserved Class 40 No D.200 climbs through Dent on 24 August 1983 with the 1600 Leeds–Carlisle. CHRISTINA SIVITER

Opposite Bottom: Duchess of Hamilton crosses Long Marton Viaduct with a southbound CME. 5 November 1983.
CHRISTINA SIVITER

Top: No 34092 storms through the cutting at the southern end of Blea Moor Tunnel with a northbound special. 7 April 1984. Note the fine Midland Railway fixed distant signal. CHRISTINA SIVITER

Above: On 27 July 1983 LNER Pacific *Flying Scotsman* hurries through Baron Wood with a southbound *Cumbrian Mountain Express.* CHRISTINA SIVITER

Top: The northern end of Blea Moor Tunnel is bathed in spring
sunshine as Class 47/4 No 47541 heads northwards with the
diverted 0810 Birmingham–Glasgow. 2 April 1983.

Night-time at Upperby, Carlisle.
Above: Union of South Africa 30 March 1984   *Below: Lord Nelson* 25 February 1984

86. *Left* LNER Pacific No 4498 *Sir Nigel Gresley* crosses Ais Gill Viaduct with the southbound CME on Wednesday 26 August 1981.

This beautiful viaduct is at an elevation of 1167 feet above sea level.

87. *Above* Elegant LNER A3 Pacific No 4472 *Flying Scotsman* climbing through the Mallerstang Valley with the SLOA special train on Sunday 30 January 1983. J. H. COOPER-SMITH

Overleaf

88. *Left* No 4472 pictured at the southern end of the 424-yard-long Birkett Tunnel with a southbound CMP on 27 July 1983. CHRIS MILNER

89. *Top right* On a hot August day (5th) in 1981 *Lord Nelson* climbs the 1 in 100 to Birkett Tunnel with a southbound CME. This splendid locomotive was built by the Southern Railway in 1926 designed by Maunsell but later modified by Bulleid. CHRIS MILNER

90. *Bottom right* Birkett Common to the north of Birkett Tunnel marks the change from moorland to pasture and meadow land. Here Merchant Navy Pacific *Clan Line* is climbing through the common with one of the return workings from the memorial service for Bishop Treacy at Appleby on 30 September 1978.

91. *Above* An interesting pairing of locomotives occurred on 3 April 1982 when SR 4-6-0 No 777 was coupled with LMS 4-6-0 No 5407. The pair are seen here heading south near Bull Gill about a mile to the north of Birkett Tunnel.

92. *Left* An unidentified Class 47 in charge of a southbound train as it climbs through Bull Gill on 3 May 1982. At this time there were still several Nottingham–Glagow trains running over this route, plus a fair amount of freight workings, but now all the freights have finished except for the Ribblehead Quarry workings and the Warcop branch pick up.

93. *Top right* *City of Wells* is photographed at Wharton Dykes climbing the last few miles to Ais Gill Summit with a southbound CME on 3 May 1982. This beautifully restored locomotive, whose home is on the famous Keighley & Worth Valley Railway, was designed by Bulleid for the Southern Railway and built in the mid 1940s.

94. *Bottom right* Wharton Dykes (just to the south of Kirkby Stephen) is the setting for this view of *Duchess of Hamilton* with a southbound CMP, on 19 March 1983. The farmhouse on the right is typical of the architecture of this part of Cumbria.

D. J. O'ROURKE

95. *Top left* Midland Compound 4-4-0 No 1000 and Jubilee Class No 5690 *Leander* (whose home is now on the Severn Valley Railway) climb away from Kirkby Stephen with a southbound special on 12 February 1983. DAVID WILCOCK

96. *Bottom left* No 46229, complete with *The Caledonian* headboard, leaving behind the station at Kirkby Stephen on a misty 11 February 1984 with a southbound CMP. This splendid locomotive seems to be having little difficulty with its thirteen coach load as it climbs the 1 in 100 up to the summit of the line at Ais Gill.

97. *Above* On a very wet August 24 1982 4-6-2 No 4498 *Sir Nigel Gresley* coasts down the 1 in 100 grade through Kirkby Stephen West with the northbound CME.

The modern looking BR style of signal box on the left had replaced the traditional Midland box some years earlier but semaphore signalling was still retained.

Overleaf
98. *Left* In this view of Kirkby Stephen West, taken on the last day of September 1983, an unidentified Class 45 locomotive races through with the light-weight 0907 Leeds–Carlisle train crossing the bridge over the A685 Brough to Tebay road.

An LMS type lattice signal dominates the right foreground, and the former goods shed and edge of the station buildings are seen on the left side of the picture.

99. *Right Duchess of Hamilton* roaring up the steep gradient through Kirkby Stephen West on 19 March 1983 with the northbound CMP. This was the occasion of its record-breaking run from Appleby to Ais Gill in a time of 23mins 55secs which, remarkably, the same locomotive bettered on the following May 30 by cutting 12secs off this time.

100. *Top left* *Duchess of Hamilton* again, this time on 7 January 1984, just north of Kirkby Stephen with a southbound CME.

Stone walls are a distinctive feature of this lovely part of England. KEN BULL

101. *Bottom left* A mile to the north of Kirkby Stephen West is the rock cutting at Waitby from which the southbound CMP hauled by 4-6-2 *City of Wells* is emerging on 20 November 1982. CHRIS MILNER

102. *Top right* High summer and bleak mid-winter are depicted in the next two views of the famous curve at Smardale – one of the finest grandstands from which to view trains on the line.

In this first picture, taken on 31 August 1982, streamlined Pacific *Sir Nigel Gresley* is seen with the southbound CME climbing the 1 in 100 round Smardale and heading for the summit of the climb at Ais Gill.

103. *Bottom right* In this scene conditions are directly opposite to those of the previous scene, as *Flying Scotsman* rounds Smardale Curve with the southbound SLOA special in blizzard conditions on 30 January 1983. KEN BULL

104. *Top left* In the author's opinion the beautifully curving Smardale Viaduct is one of the finest on the line. It has 12 spans and is 237 yards long making it the second longest viaduct on the line after Ribblehead, crossing Scandal Beck as well as the track bed of the former North Eastern line from Kirkby Stephen (NE) to Tebay.

The author was lucky here on 2 October 1982 because the train was travelling down grade at 1 in 100 but the locomotive, 4-6-0 *Sir Lamiel*, was very obligingly 'blowing off', adding considerable life to the scene. The train is a northbound special complete with *Atlantic Coast Express* headboard, a reminder of when this locomotive worked the crack expresses of the former Southern Railway.

Smardale Curve can be seen on the right as it swings away to the south-east.

105. *Bottom left* Immediately after leaving Smardale Viaduct and heading northwards the line approaches the short tunnel at Crosby Garrett. This tunnel is shown in the background as Class 47/4 No 47534 heads southwards on 25 February 1984 with the 1040 Carlisle–Leeds train, framed by a typical farm occupation bridge. Note how the right side of the top of the bridge has been darkened by the exhaust of steam trains as they climbed the 1 in 100 grade through here on the journey to Ais Gill Summit.

106. *Above* Threading the beautiful rock cutting to the north of Crosby Garrett Tunnel on 21 May 1983 is Class 31/4 No 31404 with the morning Carlisle to Leeds train. Stone from this cutting was used in the building of Crosby Garrett Viaduct. DAVID WILCOCK

107. *Above* 4-6-0 No 777 *Sir Lamiel* hauling a southbound CMP over the elegant 110 yard long viaduct at Crosby Garrett on May 22 1982.

108. *Top right* No 46229 makes a fine sight as it roars through the site of Crosby Garrett Station with the southbound CME on 11 February 1984. *The Caledonian* headboard is a reminder of the locomotive's former days of glory on the Euston–Glasgow main line.
K. J. C. JACKSON

109. *Bottom right* Class 47/3 No 47377 heading south over the short viaduct at Griseburn with a diverted Glasgow–Red Bank parcels train on Sunday 26 February 1984. This viaduct, some two miles to the north of Crosby Garrett, spans the Potts Beck.

110. *Top left* *City of Wells* has left the southern portal of Helm Tunnel and is seen here climbing the curve at Breaks Hall with a southbound CMP on 3 May 1982. This tunnel is 571 yards long and is named after the nearby hamlet of Helm. D. J. O'ROURKE

111. *Bottom left* Winter sunshine highlighting the 0907 Leeds–Carlisle train as it leaves the northern end of Helm Tunnel on a frosty 10 December 1983. The locomotive hauling the train is Class 45 No 45117.

Within a few minutes of here the train will be arriving at Appleby, one of the major towns on the route and the former county town of Westmorland.

112. *Above* 'Look Dad, there's a train' could well be the title of this picture as *Duchess of Hamilton* climbs up to Helm Tunnel with a southbound special on 7 January 1984.

Overleaf

113. *Top left* Great Ormside is the setting for *Flying Scotsman* climbing southwards with the splendid SLOA Pullman train. The date of this glorious summer's day is 29 June 1983. The train is about to cross over the road to the village of Great Ormside, which is a spur off the Appleby–Soulby road.

114. The splendid viaduct at Ormside has 10 arches, is 200 yards long and 90 feet high. Cross Fell dominates the background as *City of Wells* forges south over the viaduct on 10 December 1983.

115. *Top right* 4-6-0 *Sir Lamiel* leaves the ancient town of Appleby behind as it climbs to the south with the CMP on 4 December 1982. From here onwards the locomotive will face some very stiff climbs on the 18-mile stretch before the summit at Ais Gill is reached. The location of this shot is where the line crosses the old A66 Appleby–Brough road. CHRIS MILNER

116. *Bottom right* Class 5 4-6-0 No 5407 pulls out of Appleby with a southbound CMP on 24 August 1983 and approaches the Express Dairy, where once there were sidings for a 'Milk to London' service.

Note the Midland Railway trespass board on the left of the picture. CHRIS MILNER

117. *Above* There are still some very fine semaphore signals at Appleby, as witnessed in this picture of No 5305 leaving Appleby Station with a southbound *Santa Steam Special* on 29 December 1983.

D. J. O'ROURKE

118. *Top right* This picture, looking south from the station footbridge at Appleby, presents a good view of the splendid buildings on the down platform and shows a fair number of passengers waiting to board the 0907 Leeds–Carlisle train which is entering the station on 17 August 1983 hauled by Class 31/4 No 31406. To the rear of the train is the former goods shed now used as a small works.

119. *Bottom right* On the same day as the previous picture, Class 40 No 40122/D200 pauses at Appleby with the 1040 Carlisle–Leeds train. This preserved Class 40 locomotive with its splendid green livery was a regular performer on this route in the summer of 1983. The fine footbridge adds a touch of splendour to the scene.

120. *Top* On 28 March 1981 *Duchess of Hamilton* is pictured at the south end of Appleby Station receiving attention before leaving with the CME. Nearly all *Cumbrian Mountain* trains (both north and southbound) stop here to take water and for photographic runpasts.

121. *Above* A visual reminder of the memorial service for Bishop Eric Treacy which was held at Appleby on 30 September 1978.

The Reverend Eric Treacy, former Bishop at Wakefield, collapsed and died at Appleby on 13 May 1978 while waiting to photograph *Evening Star* on a northbound special train.

TOM HEAVYSIDE

Part Three
Appleby to Carlisle

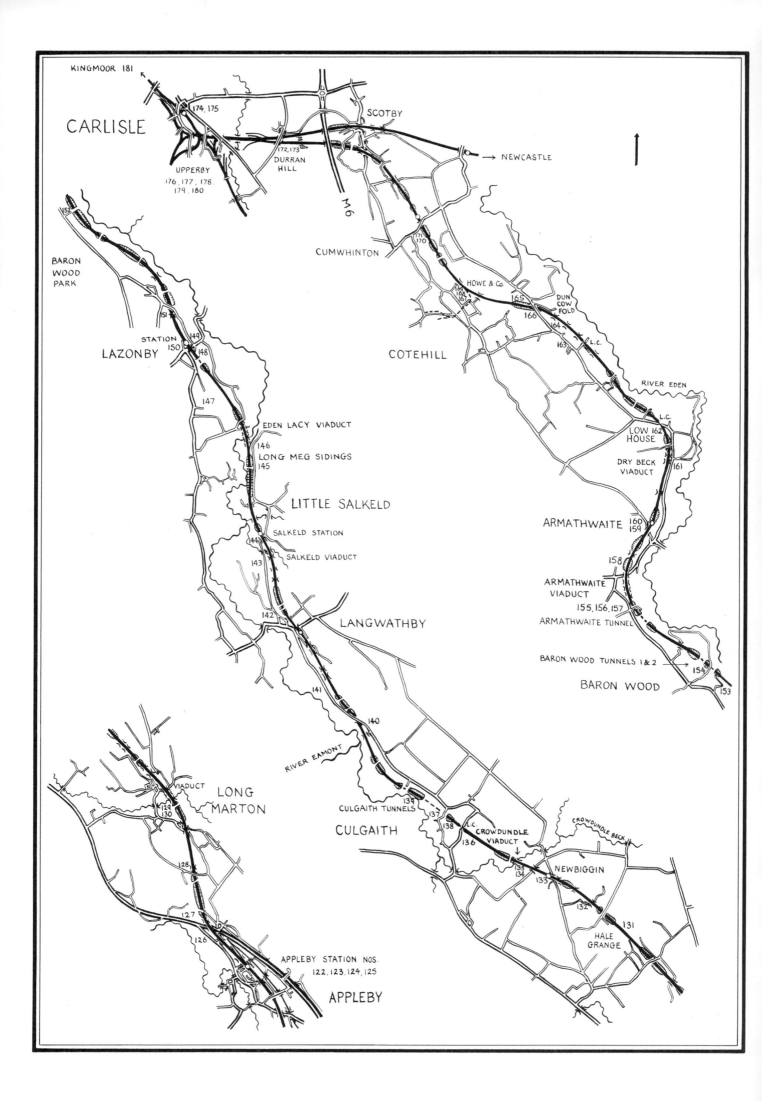

Appleby to Carlisle

Departing from Appleby the line passes under the splendid footbridge and past the signal box and branch for Warcop on the right, which reverses south between the station and the new bypass. The Ais Gill line shortly crosses over this bypass, then under an occupation bridge marking the route of the ancient Roman road. The line runs parallel with the A66 and the River Eden for a few miles, at the foot of Dufton Fells, the dark cone of Dufton Pike standing out conspicuously from the lower slopes of the fells.

Long Marton boasts a beautiful viaduct across Trout Beck (see jacket picture); its native red and white sandstone was quarried at nearby Dufton Wood. The line passes another quarry at Stamp Hill, where an aerial ropeway leads to a works at Hale Grange, near Kirkby Thore.

The valley continues to widen and support woods and arable farmland. After passing the former station at Newbiggin, the line crosses Crowdundle Beck on four graceful arches and plunges into a deep cleft. An occupation bridge spans this wooded ravine, supported by remarkably tall piers of red sandstone. A mile further on, the level crossing at Culgaith Station is encountered and the signalmen are kept busy looking after both the crossing and the two short tunnels ahead – Green Houses (or Culgaith) and Waste Bank; a lane runs over the lip of the first tunnel and meets the line again after the second tunnel. The line now threads through gently rolling fields and watermeadows and, by the confluence of the Eamont and Eden, that same lane crosses the tracks yet again.

After a couple of miles the line crosses the A686 at Langwathby close by the old station, now derelict. Nearing Little Salkeld Station the train runs over embankments and a viaduct near a cluster of mills. The hill behind the village is called 'Long Meg and her Daughters' after the ancient standing stones there. The sidings for a mine at its foot take this name and there is a modern box, now closed, and semaphores. Immediately afterwards the line bursts out of the cutting on to Eden Lacey Viaduct over the river. To the west there is a curious little hill (spot height 393 feet) which gives an excellent view to photographers of this viaduct.

Lazonby Station is reached by a tunnel which the constructors dug to avoid disturbing the rectory. The churchyard with a tall celtic cross overlooks the platforms. The station buildings now accommodate a local industry. There is a water crane at the north end of the down platform, but its tower no longer survives.

Soon after Lazonby, rail and river descend together through the Eden Gorge, in which, at Baronwood Park, you may see a herd of Highland cattle grazing near the track. The line now plunges into silver birch plantations, past a sand quarry and through two short tunnels in Baron Wood, with a very tight and precipitous gap between them. On emerging, passengers can see the cliffs overhanging the river on the north-east side. A mile further Armathwaite Tunnel is reached, amd from there the line runs out on to the massive embankment of Armathwaite Curve. Photographers waiting here are often given false hope by the roar of the nearby rapids. The curve leads on to the impressive viaduct, from where the track rises to a summit at Armathwaite Station, now disused, with its signal box, only recently abandoned, standing in a grove of pine trees opposite the old goods shed.

The gorge now widens out to the north, with the line hugging the side and hidden in trees, to emerge on Drybeck Viaduct with a roadside cottage at its foot, and thence over High Stand Gill Viaduct. Soon after, the train beats a tattoo over the second of the line's still active level crossings at Low House, where there is a box, semaphores and modern rising gates. The land now widens into spreading fields affording expansive views across the valley, until Duncowfold where the approach to the road bridge is flanked by lines of pine trees and a platelayers' hut.

In a mile on open ground stands the working signal box at Howe & Company's siding, reached by winding lanes traversing old level crossings, where a branch had run to a factory at Cocklakes, and some of the old tracks have been lifted and given to a preserved line. Locomotives on *Cumbrian Mountain Specials* sometimes change here to save time going in to Carlisle Station. The next station at Cumwhinton still stands, now let and fenced-off, and is clearly seen from the road bridge. The train now passes the line's last village of Scotby over a viaduct buried in trees. After ducking under the M6, the S & C meets the line from Newcastle at Durran Hill, close by a conspicuous TV transmitter; here the site of the old sidings can be identified by an expanse of overgrown ballast.

At last the journey ends under the electric catenaries in Carlisle Citadel; locomotives detached from the train can now go their separate ways: steam engines doubling back on to the Penrith line for stabling at Upperby, while diesels cross the river to the Kingmoor depot.

Previous Page

122. *Top left* Class 40 No 40185 photographed at the north end of Appleby Station on 21 May 1983, reversing a Stranraer–Warcop troop special on to the line to Appleby East from where it will proceed forward down the former North Eastern line which now terminates at Warcop. This line, which used to run through to Kirkby Stephen (NE), sees regular freight working specifically for the army camp at Warcop. DAVID WILCOCK

123. *Bottom left* The admiring passengers gather round to photograph No 5407 as it pauses at Appleby with a northbound CME on 7 September 1982.

124. *Top right* Class 25/2 No 25239 coasts into Appleby on Friday 30 September 1983 with the Warcop branch train from Carlisle. After pausing in the station it will then reverse down the line on the left hand side of the picture towards Appleby East and then proceed to Warcop. Note the beautiful station footbridge.

125. *Bottom right* The signalman at Appleby North box gets a grandstand view of West Country Pacific *City of Wells* under way from Appleby with a northbound CMP on 30 April 1984.
D. J. O'ROURKE

126. *Above* Class 5 4-6-0 No 5407 heading a northbound CMP and making good progress as it leaves Appleby behind and travels through the rich meadow land to the north of the ancient town. The date is 17 August 1983.

127. *Top right* Skirting the north east of Appleby is the new bypass A66 trunk road from Penrith to Scotch Corner. This photograph of 15 May 1982 shows *Sir Lamiel* in charge of a northbound CMP crossing the new bypass which is half a mile or so to the north of Appleby Station. TOM HEAVYSIDE

128. *Bottom right* A pleasant winter scene at Keld, some two miles to the north of Appleby, as *Flying Scotsman* strolls southwards with a SLOA special train on 30 January 1983. ROGER HILL

129. *Above* An oak tree provides a perfect frame for *Duchess of Hamilton* as it hurries a southbound special over Long Marton Viaduct on 5 November 1983. This viaduct crosses Trout Beck, a tributary of the river Eden, and was constructed of sandstone quarried at nearby Dufton Wood.

130. *Top right* Another view of Long Marton Viaduct. The train is the 1540 Carlisle–Leeds train hauled by an unidentified Class 31 locomotive on 26 March 1983. Snow-capped Cross Fell provides an attractive backcloth and Trout Beck is in the left foreground of the picture.

131. *Bottom right* Pictured at Hale Grange, to the north of Long Marton, on Sunday 31 July 1983 is the *Hadrian Pullman* from Kings Cross to Carlisle hauled by English Electric Class 40 locomotive No D200. The factory is the British Gypsum works, which has an aerial ropeway to the mine at Stamp Hill. DAVID WILCOCK

132. *Top left* This splendid oak tree dominates the scene at Hale Grange, half a mile to the north of the previous picture's location, as 4-6-0 No 5305 speeds southwards with the *Santa Steam Special* of 29 December 1983. BRIAN DOBBS

133. *Bottom left* Passing the disused station at Newbiggin on a summer's day – 27 July 1983 – is LNER Pacific *Flying Scotsman* with a southbound CMP. Although the station is out of use, the clock remains and there is still glass in some of the window frames. K. J. C. JACKSON

134. *Above* In winter sunshine *City of Wells*, hauling a southbound CMP, crosses Crowdundle Viaduct on 10 December 1983. This four-arch viaduct, situated at Newbiggin, is 86 yards long, 55 feet high and crosses Crowdundle Beck – the old boundary between Westmorland and Cumberland.

Overleaf

135. *Top left* A climb of around 1 in 200 faces southbound trains between Culgaith and Newbiggin and in this picture *Duchess of Hamilton*, framed by a beautiful occupation bridge, approaches Crowdundle Viaduct with the southbound *Thames–Eden Pullman* on 23 April 1983. D. J. O'ROURKE

136. *Bottom left* LMS Jubilee Class 4-6-0 No 5690 *Leander* about to beat a tattoo on Culgaith Crossing as it hurries south past the remains of the old station with the *Jubilee* special on 26 April 1980. Although there are modern barriers here there are still an original Midland signal box and semaphore signals.

137. *Right* A bird's eye view of Culgaith Crossing taken from above Culgaith Tunnel and looking south, showing a northbound special hauled by No 25035 and No 31102 on 5 November 1983. The site of the station can be seen in this view. D. J. O'ROURKE

138. *Above* Class 5 4-6-0- No 5407 running out of the 661-yard-long Culgaith Tunnel with a southbound CME on 2 September 1981. This tunnel has a single ventilation shaft of 74 feet depth.

139. *Right* Midland Compound No 1000 and *Leander* photographed heading south on 12 February 1983 with a CMP. The location is between Waste Bank and Culgaith Tunnels. Waste Bank is an extremely short tunnel and was originally planned as a cutting. J. H. COOPER-SMITH

Overleaf

140. *Top left* *Sir Nigel Gresley* races through the Eden Valley (to the north of Culgaith) with a southbound CME on 15 July 1981. From here to Cotehill, some seventeen miles to the north, the line and the River Eden are never more than a mile apart. This photograph was taken where the Rivers Eamont and Eden meet.

141. *Bottom left* *Flying Scotsman* hurries through the rich farmland of the Eden Valley with a northbound CMP on a hazy summer day – 22 June 1983. The exact location is High Barn, a mile south of Langwathby.

142. *Top right* Class 5 No 5305 approaches Langwathy with the southbound *Santa Steam Special* on 29 December 1983. Little Salkeld Viaduct, crossing the Briggle Beck, is at the top left of the picture. This viaduct is 134 yards long, is 60 feet high and has seven spans. At one time the village of Langwathby played a very important part in the Midland Railway's bid for traffic to and from the important town of Penrith, some five miles to the south west.

143. *Bottom right* *City of Wells* heading into the winter sunshine with a southbound CMP on 20 November 1982. The train has just left Little Salkeld Viaduct and is climbing upgrade towards Langwathby. K. J. C. JACKSON

144. *Top* LNER Pacific *Flying Scotsman* in charge of a SLOA private charter train, running through Little Salkeld Station on 30 January 1983. Although the station is now out of use the fine Midland buildings remain and the platforms still look in good order. BRIAN DOBBS

145. *Above* Just to the north of Little Salkeld Station are Long Meg Sidings which served the nearby anhydrite works and here a SLOA private charter train, headed by *Flying Scotsman* is storming southwards through the sidings on 30 January 1983. Beyond Little Salkeld Station, on the east side of the line, is a hill on top of which is a set of ancient stones – Long Meg and her Daughters! 'Long Meg' is a square stone with its four corners coinciding with the main points of the compass and the 'Daughters' are sixty-six smaller stones that are arranged in circular form. D. J. O'ROURKE

146. *Top* No 34092 *City of Wells* approaching Long Meg Sidings on 10 December 1983 with a southbound CMP. At this point the train has just travelled over Eden Lacy or Long Meg Viaduct. The signalling in this section is a mixture of modern colour lights and, as can be seen in this picture, traditional semaphores.

D. J. O'ROURKE

147. *Above* In this photograph, taken from the hillside to the west of the line, No 4498 *Sir Nigel Gresley* crosses Eden Lacy Viaduct with a southbound special on 2 October 1982. This viaduct, which crosses the River Eden, is 137 yards long and 60 feet high.

148. *Top left* *Lord Nelson* storming out of the 99 yard long tunnel at Lazonby with a northbound CME on 25 February 1984. Lazonby Tunnel was originaly planned as a cutting, but because the line was so close to the rectory the Church authorities insisted on it being a tunnel.

150. *Above* There was still a Midland Railway water crane at the end of the down platform at Lazonby when this photograph was taken on 20 July 1983. The train is the 1635 Carlisle–Leeds hauled by Class 31/4 No 31411. The goods shed and buildings on the left are now used by a local bakery. K. J. C. JACKSON

149. *Bottom left* *City of Wells* racing through Lazonby with a northbounbd CMP on 30 April 1983. The roof of the rectory, mentioned in the previous caption, can be seen above the third and fourth coaches. The road in the foreground is the B6413 from Brampton to Plumpton on the A6.

151. *Top left* Class 9F 2-10-0 *Evening Star* running out of Lazonby with the northbound *Lord Bishop* special train on 30 September 1978. TOM HEAVYSIDE

152. *Bottom left* After leaving Lazonby the line runs northwards through the beautiful Eden Gorge traversing Baron Wood. Heading south through the southern end of Baron Wood is *Flying Scotsman* with the CMP on 27 July 1983.

153. *Above* Class 40 No 40028 heading north on 23 April 1983 with the stock for a *Cumbrian Mountain Pullman*. The photograph was taken a few hundred yards to the north of the previous picture's location, with the Eden Gorge in the background. CHRIS MILNER

154. *Left* On the stretch of line between Baron Wood and Armathwaite there are three tunnels. From south to north they are Baron Wood No 1 (207 yards), Baron Wood No 2 (251 yards) and Armathwaite (325 yards). In this picture we see No 5690 *Leander* leaving Baron Wood No 2 Tunnel with a southbound special on 3 July 1980. J. H. COOPER-SMITH

155. *Above* An unidentified Class 47 has just rounded Armathwaite Curve and is heading for Armathwaite Tunnel on Sunday 26 February 1984 with the diverted 0930 Carlisle–Euston train.

Overleaf
156 & 157. *Top and bottom left* Armathwaite Curve provides the perfect grandstand from which to view southbound steam trains. In the first view we see *Leander* heading south with a CMP on a sunny 23 January 1982. The second photograph, taken from a similar position a few weeks later (27 February), shows *Duchess of Hamilton* in fine form heading a southbound CMP. At this position both trains have just left Armathwaite Viaduct.

158. *Right* Weak winter sunshine highlights Class 45 No 45055 *Royal Corps of Transport* as it leaves the curving 176-yard nine-arched Armathwaite Viaduct and heads north with a special from Kings Cross. The train will stop at Howe & Company's Siding (some five miles to the north) where *Duchess of Hamilton* will replace the *Peak* locomotive for its return journey to the south via the S & C. That is the reason why so many cars are parked on the road in the background, with people positioning themselves to view the return journey at Armathwaite Curve. 7 January 1984.

159. *Top left City of Wells* approaches Armathwaite Station with a southbound special on 13 February 1982.

160. *Bottom left* English Electric Class 40 No D200 hurrying through Armathwaite with the 1600 Leeds–Carlisle on 17 August 1983. The Midland signal box remains (although out of use) and the edge of the old goods shed frames the right side of the picture. At the end of the train can be seen the up platform of the now closed station at Armathwaite.

161. *Top* Just north of Armathwaite is one of the heaviest embankments on the line (containing some 400,000 cubic feet of materials), with the short Dry Beck Viaduct in the middle. Heading south with a CMP on 31 October 1981 is *Duchess of Hamilton*. K. J. C. JACKSON

162. *Above Sir Lamiel* running through Low House Crossing with a southbound CMP on 22 May 1982. This is one of only two level crossings on the line, the first one being at Culgaith. Both now have the modern barrier type of gates.

Previous pages

163. *Top left* A wintry scene at Duncowfold near Cotehill as *Flying Scotsman* hurries by with the SLOA special on 30 January 1983.

164. *Bottom left* 4-6-0 No 777 *Sir Lamiel* climbs the 1 in 132 at Cotehill with a southbound CMP on 4 December 1982. ROGER HILL

165. *Top right* Heading north at Cotehill on the morning of 7 January 1984 is Class 45 No 45109 with the 0907 Leeds–Carlisle train. Note the platelayers' hut and how the trees have been affected by the prevailing winds. The mileage marker on the up line reminds the traveller that there are still 302 miles to go to St. Pancras. The complete distance from Carlisle to London is 308 miles.

166. *Bottom right* Nos 1000 and 5690 caught in action as they head south between Howe's Siding and Cotehill on 12 February 1983. CHRIS MILNER

167. *Above* *Sir Lamiel* in charge of a southbound CMP makes a fine sight as it rounds the curve at Howe & Company's Siding on 4 December 1982. The fine signal box is still open although the private sidings for the local works have been taken up but, happily, have been given to a preservation line. The spur to the siding can be seen immediately to the right of the signal box.

168. *Top right* Class 40 No 40177 rounding the curves at Howe's Siding is proceeding northwards with the return working of the Carlisle–Appleby/Warcop morning pick-up freight on 24 August 1983. These English Electric locomotives were first introduced in 1958, and after starting out their lives hauling the crack expresses on the East and West Coast main lines, they are now relegated to, in the main, secondary duties, or, sadly, being scrapped.

169. *Bottom right* *Duchess of Hamilton* with a southbound CMP makes a splendid sight as it storms past Howe's Siding on 27 February 1982. D. J. O'ROURKE

Previous pages

170. *Top left* Although Cunwhinton Station, to the north of Howe's Siding, was closed in 1952 it still has a well preserved look about it. Nos 1000 and 5690 make a handsome pair as they head south through the station on their journey to Howe's Siding where they will wait to work the *Cumbrian Mountain Pullman* south to Hellifield on 12 February 1982.

171. *Bottom left* In the previous picture Cumwhinton Station was to let. In this photograph of a special DMU working from Workington to Leeds on 7 January 1984 it is obvious from the work that has been going on that the station building has now, happily, been occupied.

172. *Top right* A mile to the north of Cumwhinton the line travels through the village of Scotby. It then passes under the M6 motorway and arrives at Durran Hill where it meets the line from Newcastle. In this view of Durran Hill, where there were once extensive sidings, Nos 777 and 5407 head south with a CMP. The Newcastle line is visible on the right of the picture just below the industrial diesel shunter.

173. *Bottom right* In this view, taken from the same spot as the previous picture, *City of Wells*, in charge of a southbound CMP, is seen running through the western approach to the City of Carlisle. Durran Hill was where the Midland Railway had its locomotive depot. ROGER HILL

174. *Top left* No D200 reverses the stock of the 1600 Leeds–Carlisle train out of Carlisle Citadel Station on 23 August 1983. This grand station, which was once host to many different railway companies, still retains an air of Victorian elegance and splendour.

175. *Bottom left* A splendid line-up of motive power at Carlisle on 22 March 1980. From left to right Class 46 No 46009 waiting to take over a Glasgow–Nottingham train, Class 83 electric locomotive stabled, and Class 5 4-6-0 No 5305 waiting to leave with the southbound CME. K. J. C. JACKSON

176. *Above* Carlisle Upperby is the stabling point or shed for steam locomotives that work the *Cumbrian Mountain* trains. In this view *City of Wells* receives attention at Upperby after working in with a northbound CMP on 30 April 1983.

Previous page
Four night scenes at Carlisle Upperby.
177. *Top left* *Duchess of Hamilton* on 6 January 1984.
178. *Bottom left* Class 5 No 5305 on 28 December 1983.
179. *Top right* No 5690 *Leander* on 11 February 1983.
180. *Bottom right* Midland Compound No 1000 on
11 February 1983.

181. *Above* Class 40 No 40052 pokes its head out of Carlisle
Kingmoor depot on 30 April 1983. Kingmoor is where all the
diesel locomotives that work on the Settle & Carlisle are serviced
and maintained.